A Day in the Life: Desert Animals

Gila Monster

Anita Ganeri

www.raintreepublishers.co.uk
Visit our website to find out
more information about
Raintree books.

To order:
☎ Phone 0845 6044371
🖷 Fax +44 (0) 1865 312263
🖳 Email myorders@raintreepublishers.co.uk

Customers from outside the UK please telephone +44 1865 312262

Raintree is an imprint of Capstone Global Library Limited,
a company incorporated in England and Wales having
its registered office at 7 Pilgrim Street, London, EC4V 6LB
– Registered company number: 6695582

Edited by Daniel Nunn, Rebecca Rissman, and Sian Smith
Designed by Richard Parker
Picture research by Elizabeth Alexander
Production by Victoria Fitzgerald
Originated by Capstone Global Library Ltd
Printed and bound in China by South China Printing
 Company Ltd

ISBN 978 1 406 21962 3 (hardback)
14 13 12 11 10
10 9 8 7 6 5 4 3 2 1

**British Library Cataloguing in Publication
Data**
Ganeri, Anita, 1961-
  Gila monster. -- (A day in the life. Desert animals)
  1. Gila monster--Juvenile literature.
  I. Title II. Series
  597.9'5952-dc22

Acknowledgements
We would like to thank the following for permission to
reproduce photographs: Alamy pp. 7, 23 glossary desert
(© Andrew Harrington), 8 (© Design Pics Inc.), 12 (©
Roberto Nistri), 10 (© Rick & Nora Bowers); Corbis pp.
17, 23 glossary poison (© Kennan Ward); FLPA p. 14 (©
ZSSD/Minden Pictures); Getty Images pp. 16 (Barbara
Jordan/Photographer's Choice), 18, 21 (Jim Merli/Visuals
Unlimited); © Jack Goldfarb p. 22; Photolibrary pp. 4, 9,
20, 23 glossary scales (John Cancalosi/age fotostock), 13
(Matt Meadows/Peter Arnold Images), 11, 23 glossary
burrow (C. Allan Morgan/Peter Arnold Images), 15,
23 glossary predator (Marty Cordano/OSF), 19 (PAUL
FREED/Animals Animals); Shutterstock pp. 5, 23 glossary
reptile (© Susan Flashman), 23 glossary insect (© Anke van
Wyk), 23 glossary prey (© EcoPrint).

Front cover photograph of an adult Gila monster
(Heloderma suspectum) basking at the mouth of its den
reproduced with permission of Photolibrary (Wayne Lynch/
All Canada Photos).

Back cover photograph of (left) a Gila monster's scales
reproduced with permission of Photolibrary (John
Cancalosi/age fotostock); and (right) a Gila monster
somewhere in southwestern North America, CA reproduced
with permission of Corbis (© Kennan Ward).

We would like to thank Michael Bright for his assistance in
the preparation of this book.

Contents

Some words are shown in bold, **like this**.
You can find them in the glossary on page 23.

What is a Gila monster?

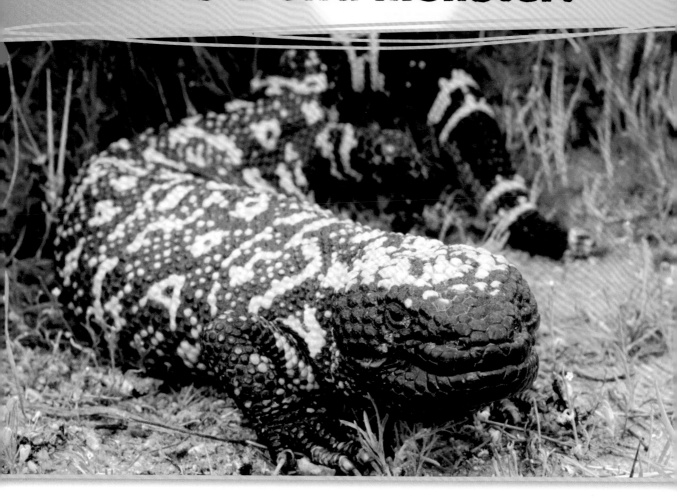

A Gila monster is a lizard.

You say Gila as "HEE-la".

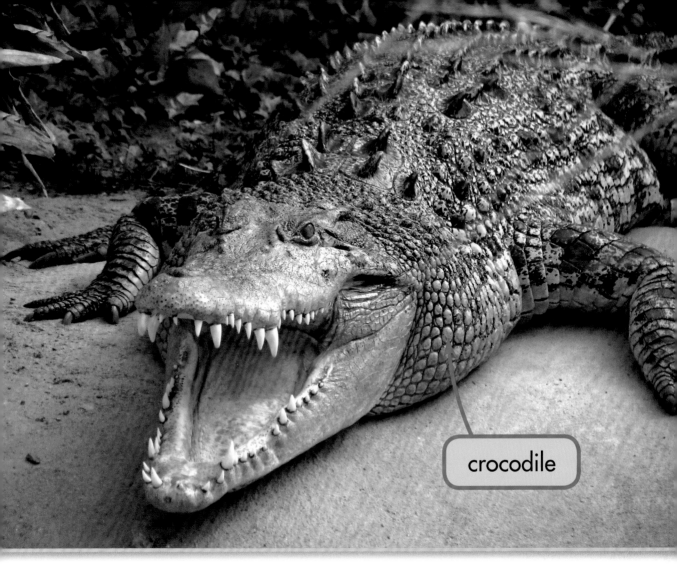

crocodile

Gila monsters belong to a group of animals called **reptiles**.

Crocodiles and snakes are also reptiles.

Where do Gila monsters live?

United States

Mexico

deserts

Gila monsters live in the **deserts** of the south-west United States and northern Mexico.

Can you find these deserts on the map?

In the day, it is hot in the desert but it gets cooler at night.

Gila monsters dig **burrows** in the sand or live in burrows dug by other animals.

What do Gila monsters look like?

Gila monsters have big, heavy bodies, with short, fat tails.

They can grow to be as long as your arm.

scale

A Gila monster's body is covered in black, pink, and yellow **scales**.

The scales look like small, round beads.

What do Gila monsters do in the day?

In spring, the weather is cooler in the **desert**.

Gila monsters spend most of the day looking for food.

burrow

In summer, it is very hot during the day.

Gila monsters stay in their **burrows** out of the sun.

What do Gila monsters do at night?

In spring, Gila monsters spend the night resting in their **burrows**.

They come out in the morning to go hunting again.

In summer, it is cooler in the **desert** at night.

Gila monsters come out at night to look for food.

What do Gila monsters eat?

Gila monsters use smell to find their food, by flicking their tongues in and out.

They eat birds, eggs, mice, **insects**, and other lizards.

A Gila monster bites its **prey** with its powerful jaws to kill it.

Then the Gila monster swallows it whole.

How do Gila monsters defend themselves?

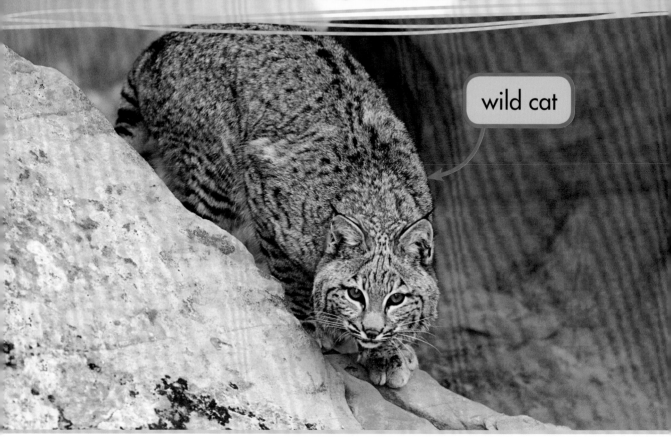

wild cat

If Gila monsters are out in the day or night, they have to watch out for **predators**.

Coyotes, hawks, dogs, and wild cats hunt Gila monsters.

If a predator comes close, the Gila monster opens its mouth and hisses.

Then it bites and chews its **poison** into its attacker.

Where are baby Gila monsters born?

egg

In summer, the female digs a hole in the ground and lays her eggs in it.

She buries them and goes away.

Next spring, the eggs hatch and the babies crawl out.

They look like little adults and can already look after themselves.

What do Gila monsters do in winter?

In winter, it gets cold in the **desert**.

Gila monsters stay in their **burrows** and go into a deep sleep.

tail

The Gila monsters do not need to eat in winter.

They live off fat stored in their tails until they wake up again next spring.

Gila monster body map

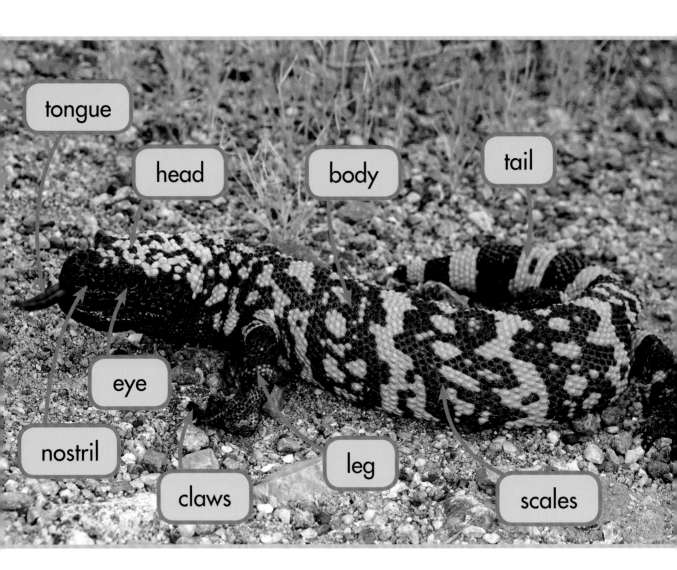

tongue

head

body

tail

eye

nostril

leg

claws

scales

Glossary

 burrow hole in the ground where an animal lives

 desert very dry place that is rocky, stony, or sandy

 insect animal that has six legs, such as a grasshopper

 poison something that can cause illness or death

 predator animal that hunts other animals for food

 prey animal that is eaten by other animals

 reptile animal with scaly skin, such as a lizard or snake

 scales tiny flaps of hard skin on a reptile's body

Find out more

Books

Desert Animals (Focus on Habitats), Stephen Savage (Wayland, 2006)

Deserts (My World of Geography), Angela Royston (Heinemann Library, 2004)

24 Hours: Desert (Focus on Habitats), Elizabeth Haldane (Dorling Kindersley, 2006)

Websites

Learn more about Gila monsters at:
kids.yahoo.com/animals/reptiles/4420--Gila+Monster

Look at photos of Gila monsters and find out about them at:
www.sandiegozoo.org/animalbytes/t-gila_monster.html

Index